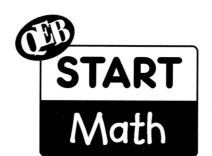

Sizes and Shapes

Book 1

Ann Montague-Smith

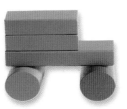

QEB Publishing

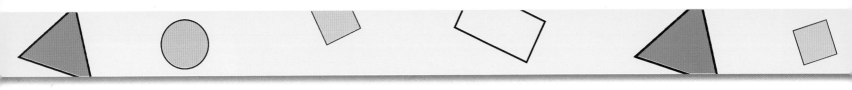

Published in the United States by
QEB Publishing, Inc.
23062 La Cadena Drive
Laguna Hills, CA 92653

www.qeb-publishing.com

Library of Congress Control Number: 2004102068

ISBN 1-59566-155-7

Written by Ann Montague-Smith
Designed and edited by The Complete Works
Illustrated by Jenny Tulip
Photography by Steve Lumb and Michael Wicks

Creative Director Louise Morley
Editorial Manager Jean Coppendale

Printed and bound in China

With thanks to:

Contents

Cubes and spheres

Point to the cubes.

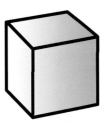

cube

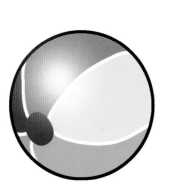

Point to the spheres.

sphere

Challenge

Find some building blocks. See if you can pick out all the cubes.

Pyramids and cones

Point to the cones.

cone

Use some pyramid and cone building blocks.
Make some more trees for the picture.

Point to the pyramids.

pyramid

Challenge

Find some cubes, spheres, cones, and pyramids. Make a house for the picture. Which shapes work best? Why do you think that?

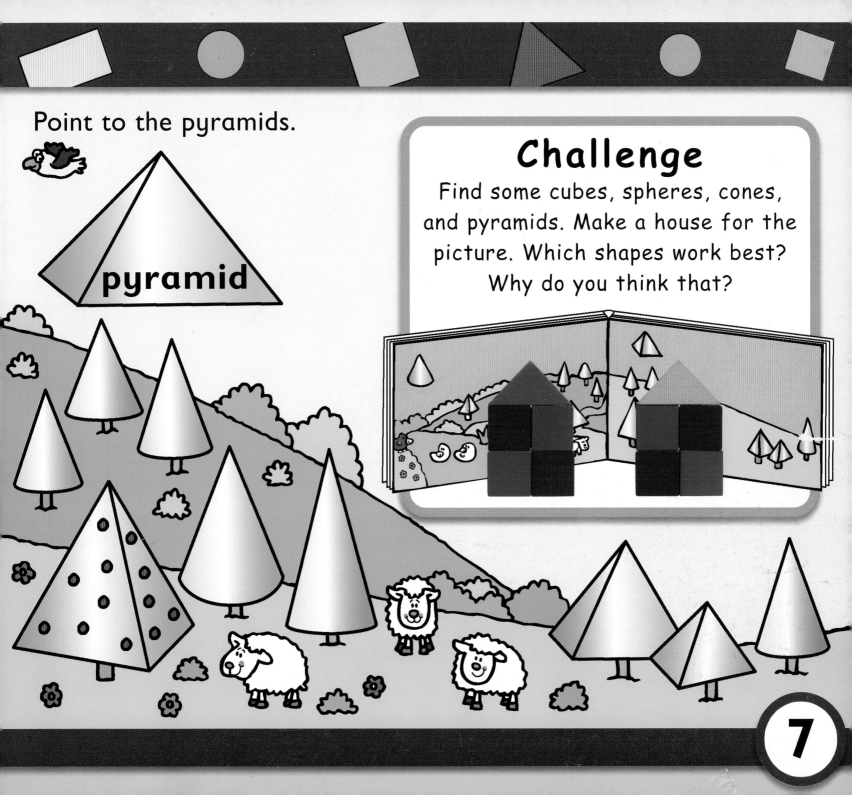

Match the shapes that are the same.

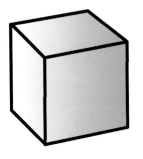  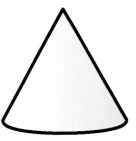  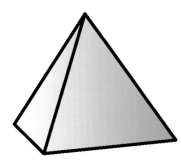

cube　　**sphere**　　**cone**　　**pyramid**

Say the names of the shapes.

Challenge

Find a cone and a pyramid.
Get some paper and paint.
Print with the cone and
the pyramid.
What shapes can you see?

9

Squares and circles

Get some red and blue tokens.

Put a red token on each square.

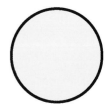 **square** 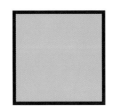 **circle**

Put a blue token on each circle.

Challenge

Get some colored paper squares and circles. Make your own people from these shapes.

Triangles and rectangles

Point to the triangles.

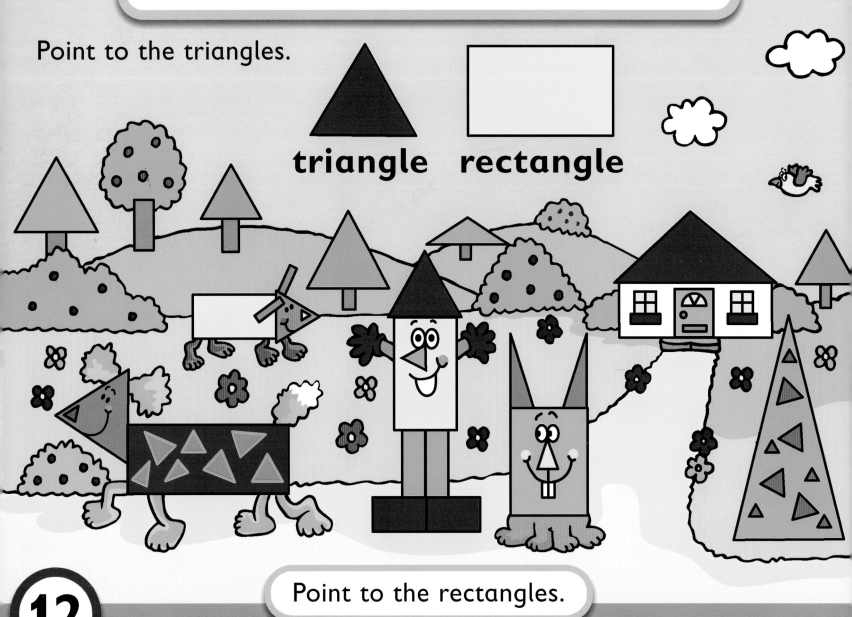

triangle   rectangle

Point to the rectangles.

12

Challenge

Find some triangle and rectangle shapes. Make your own animals with these shapes.

Make a picture

Get some square, rectangle, triangle, and circle shapes. Use the shapes to make the pictures.

Which shapes did you use to make your pictures?

Challenge

Make your own picture using squares, rectangles, triangles, and circles.

Up and down

Two of you play this game with 3 tokens. Take turns to throw a token onto the chooser. Move your token to the next square with the chooser shape on it. Move up a ladder and down a hose if you land on them. The winner is the first one to reach the finish.

start

finish

17

Challenge

Find a friend, a dollhouse,
and a toy chair. Ask your
friend to shut her eyes.
Put the chair in the dollhouse
and say where it is.
Ask your friend to open her eyes.
Can she find the chair?

Where is it?

Point to the top of the jungle gym.

What is at the bottom of the slide?

Where would you like to play?

What would you do?

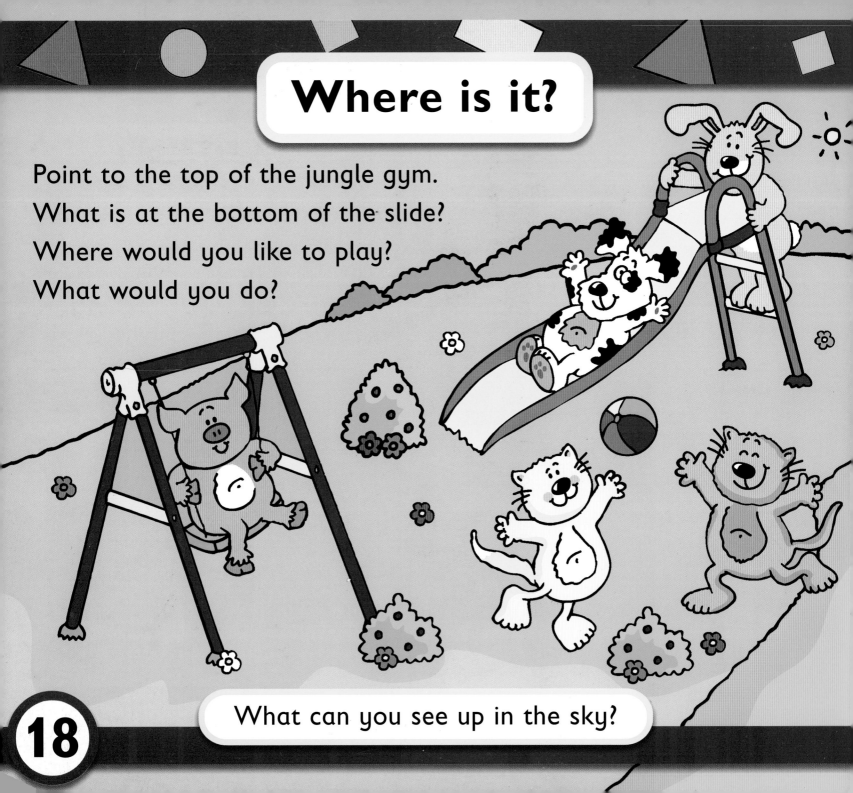

What can you see up in the sky?

Challenge

Play "I Spy" with a friend. Look around the room. Say, "I spy something on top of the cabinet." Ask your friend to guess what the object is. When your friend has answered you, it's then your friend's turn to play.

19

I know

Get some board game tokens. Listen to the words.
Put a token on the picture that matches each word.

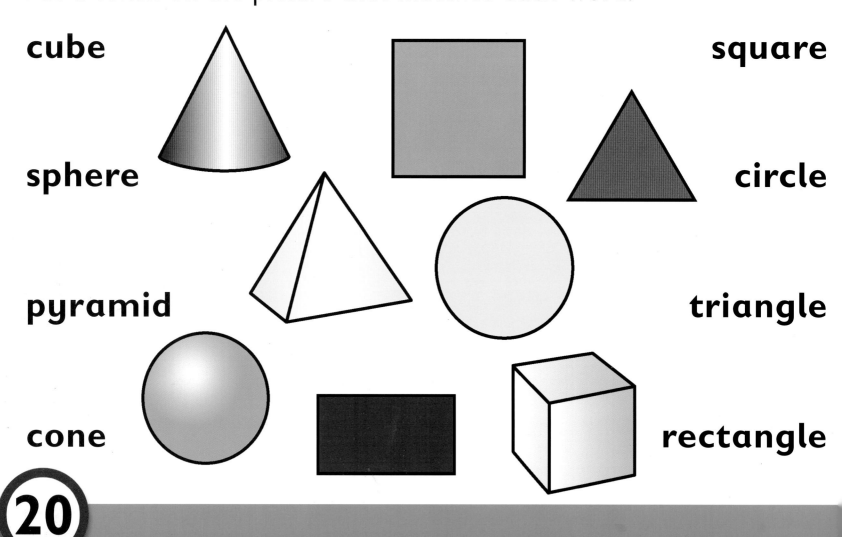

cube

sphere

pyramid

cone

square

circle

triangle

rectangle

on top

underneath

up

down

Challenge

Look around you.
Can you find the shapes on these pages?
Now look for things that are up or down.
Can you find things that are
on top or underneath?

Supporting notes for adults

Cubes and spheres – pages 4-5

At this stage, children might call these shapes "box" and "ball." Practice saying "cube" and "sphere" together.

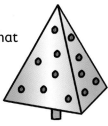

Pyramids and cones – pages 6-7

If children are unsure about cones, talk about ice cream cones. If you know of any product that comes in a pyramid-shaped box, discuss this with the children.

Shape match – pages 8-9

Encourage the children to say the names of the shapes that they see in the picture. Ask questions such as, "What is the same shape?" "What is different about these shapes?"

Squares and circles – pages 10-11

Point to the shapes at the top of the pages and say their names: "circle... square." Ask the children to practice saying these words.

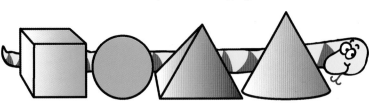

Triangles and rectangles – pages 12-13

Again, practice saying the names of these shapes. Children might confuse squares and rectangles. Provide some flat rectangle and square shapes for the children to sort, so that they begin to recognize the similarities and differences.

Make a picture – pages 14-15

If the children find it difficult to make the pictures using shapes, ask them to show you each shape in turn, for one of the pictures. Together, use these shapes to make the picture.

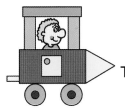

Up and down – pages 16-17

Talk about "up" and "down." If children are unsure, ask them to stretch up, then squat down. As the children play the game, ask, "Which way will you move now? Up or down?"

Where is it? – pages 18-19

Ask questions about the picture, using words such as high, low, beside, behind, on top, under… Encourage the children to say what they can see in these positions.

I know – pages 20-21

Read the shape words. Ask the children to say which shape word describes which picture. Some of the pictures will have 2 ideas, such as up and down. Encourage the children to show you which part of the picture depicts each idea.

Suggestions for using this book

Children will enjoy looking through the book and talking about the colorful pictures. Sit somewhere comfortable together. Read the instructions to the children, then encourage them to take part in the activity and check whether or not they understand what to do.

In this book, children are introduced to the solid shapes of cubes, spheres, pyramids, and cones. Encourage them to sort through building blocks to find examples of these shapes. At first, they might call a cube a "box" and a sphere a "ball." This is perfectly all right and shows that they are recognizing these mathematical shapes in everyday things.

The flat shapes introduced are squares, circles, triangles, and rectangles. Encourage children to recognize that squares are the faces of cubes, that pyramids have triangular faces, and so on. This will help to avoid confusion later on in their learning between which are solid and which are flat shapes.

Encourage the children to talk about the properties of shapes, such as which solid shapes have flat faces, and which have curved faces. This will help them distinguish the shapes.

Children will enjoy making their own models and pictures from shapes, as well as copying the ones given in the book. Encourage them to talk about which shapes would be good to make something, and why they think so.

When the children tackle each Challenge, ask questions such as, "Why do you think so? Is there another way to do this? What else could you try?"